Sheram In Love

*A colorful collection of love songs
from one of Armenia's most notable ashoughs*

2022

Sheram in Love.
A colorful collection of love songs from one of Armenia's most notable ashoughs.

No part of this publication may be reproduced, stored in or introduced into a retrieval system, or transmitted, in any form, or by any means (electronic, mechanical, photocopying, recording, or otherwise), without the prior permission of the publisher.

Requests for permission should be directed to books@dudukhouse.com.

ISBN: 978-1-7779990-5-6 (Paperback)
ISBN: 978-1-7779990-6-3 (Hardcover)

Copyright © 2022 by Dudukhouse, Inc.

www.dudukhousemusic.com

Without roots, trees cannot grow.

The project aims to preserve the legacy of Armenian ashough music.

www.dudukhousemusic.com

1857 - 1938

Ashough Sheram
(Grigor Talyan)

FROM THE PUBLISHER

With great pleasure, we announce the publication of the second book devoted to one of Armenia's most important ashughs. The focus of our attention is on Sheram as a poet of love this time.

Aside from Armenia, Ashugh Sheram (Grigor Talyan) is unknown to the outside world. There are two reasons for this: first, most of his music is traditional Armenian folk music, which has a strong resonance mostly among Armenians. Secondly, none of the songs performed by this notable ashough have been ever translated or performed in English. While translating and performing Sheram's songs in English will prove to be relatively challenging, we nevertheless provide the world with a glimpse into Sheram's mind as a poet by translating some of his songs into English in this book.

Ashough Sheram composed so many beautiful and memorable songs that are still performed today that we are confident that his music will continue to live on long after his passing in 1938. The beauty, complexity, and sometimes unconventional nature of his melodies have earned him the nickname Sheram, which refers to a silkworm. "You are weaving your melodies in a similar manner to a silkworm", was an observation by the distinguished Armenian poet Hovhannes Hovhannisyan once, resulting in the birth of his new musical avatar.

There are thirty songs by Ashough Sheram in this book, which have been translated for the first time into English. We have given up the rhymes in the translation of Sheram's poetry in order to preserve its essence and original thought form.

There are often words in Sheram song lyrics that are unfamiliar even to Armenian speakers with excellent knowledge. This is because in his language, Sheram borrowed many words from the Alexandropolol (Gyumri) dialect of Armenian. Consequently, a comprehensive dictionary with English terms is provided at the end of the book to assist readers unfamiliar with the dialect.

And finally, we have also included the musical notation of the songs as transcribed by Sheram's son, composer Vardges Talyan circa 1948. If you perform songs from this book, you may notice that the melodies of some songs differ from those you have heard previously. This is because the population has learned Sherams' songs by listening to singers (such as Araksya Gyulzadyan) rather than by studying transcriptions. Accordingly, there may have been some modifications to the melodic lines as the melodies passed from one generation to the next.

TO THE UNFORGETTABLE MEMORY OF THE POET-SINGER SHERAM

Avetik Isahakyan's introduction to the first edition (1948)

Alexandropol (Leninakan[1]) is considered a city of ashughs. My teenage years were spent counting at least thirty ashughs, or folk singers, who were quite famous all over town. Their songs and music were part of celebrations, engagement parties, weddings, and feasts throughout the city. Local ashughs even had their own cafe where they would sing and play in front of spectators. There were also other cafes where ashugh-singers from abroad regularly gathered to compete. Thus, Alexandropol created a unique ashugh atmosphere with its traditions and customs.

The youngest and most recent of the ashugh-singers of Alexandropol was the ashugh-composer Grigor Talyan, or Usta[2] Gokor. He descended from well-respected and loved musical family and was later known as the famous and beloved singer Sheram, named by the great poet Hovhannes Hovhannisyan.

Young Grigor Talyan was born and raised in that ashugh atmosphere. He learned from old masters and became proficient in ashugh art and lyrics. He was still very young when he made a name for himself and won the love of the public. He was a master tar player and an emotional singer—he lived in his music and songs. His art was heartwarming—everyone around listening to his music lived with him in that touching beauty.

---

[1] Previous names of the city of Gyumri.

[2] 2 Usta = Master, a respectful title given to people who mastered their art (e.g. musicians, artists, craftsmen) etc.

For the People of Alexandropol, Sheram was the joy and splendour of parties. With the playing of his tar, his heartfelt voice, and his love songs about jealousy, longing, and sorrow, Sheram drove the passionate youth crazy. He filled many of the young people with ambitions of love, and filled many more with poetic sadness. They eagerly awaited his new songs, and, because Sheram's creative talent was surprisingly fruitful and inexhaustible, they never waited long.

In their eyes, there was no other ashugh-singer equal to Sheram. If the residents were traveling to another city like Yerevan, or Tbilisi (Georgia) and listening to other famous ashughs, they would have remembered Sheram with nostalgia.

I remember hearing about Sheram from my youth. "Dying is nothing, but if we can't listen to Gokor, that's the pain…", "Listening to Gokor is life, it is happiness", or "Our Gokor will light a fire in a heartless person".

I know that the sweet name of Usta Gokor still lives on in the hearts of the people of Alexandropol alive today, because he has beautified and poetized their youthful days. Even after the October Revolution, in our Soviet world, Sheram's old songs live together with his new songs. Even now, his lovely songs are heard on the stage and on the radio, which, as in the old days, move our people, make them happy and excited.

Let the heartfelt songs of my dear, old friend, my youth friend, Ashugh Gokor, be heard for many, many years.

May his lyre never be forgotten.

Avetik Isahakyan
Full member of the Academy of Sciences of the Armenian SSR

A COUPLE OF WORDS

Garegin Levonyan's preface to the first edition (1948)

Poet, singer and musician Grigor Talyan (Ashugh Sheram) is one of the lucky authors whose songs are published in a complete collection with notation of their melodies.

This is the first case, and it is significant in Armenian ashough literature. Since the 1850's, our philology has been sufficiently engaged in collecting, studying and publishing ashugh songs and melodies.

Some of our musicologists have only transiently written down or recorded a few songs of famous troubadours. Many have been kept in drawers or oddly published in various editions.

At present, the notation of all these songs of Sheram belongs to his son, composer Vardges Talyan. We were assigned only to edit the texts of the songs. However, we faced a problem in that regard; it is difficult to approach the lyrics of Sheram's songs as mere verses, because they are organically connected with their melodies. The author invented his songs-melodies together, while "holding his tar on his chest". He adapted his lyrics to the melody, often ignoring the basic rules of syllable-rhyme. Another musician-poet in 18th century Constantinople wrote in a similar fashion. It was Baghdasar Dpir. He also wrote his songs by adapting them to the melodies, or, as he said, to the sounds. The poet wrote in his notes that his songs are such that the words are built on color, not the color on the words. That's why you have to see the color first and then hear the words, so that it will be delicious to listen to." Baghdasar wanted his poems to be sung strictly with the melody it has been written for.

Sheram is a great master and talented in composing melodies. None of his contemporaries have composed as many beautiful melodies—melodies excite the emotions with their bright eastern colors. The Sheram-poet is greatly diminished by Sheram-musician. Undoubtedly, he is a musician first, then a poet. However, in his poems we also see his great mastery. We hope that our musicologists will work professionally with the musical heritage left by the author and will study that heritage in detail.

Years ago, many of our famous musicians such as A. Spendiaryan, Komitas, K. Kushnaryan, A. Ter-Ghevondyan and others became interested in Sheram's songs and even transcriber a few of his songs.

We also know that in the Romanos Melikyan Music School's Research Department, musicologist Aram Kocharyan personally transcribed all his songs from Sheram and prepared a special scientific work.

BIOGRAPHY

Grigor Talyan (Ashugh Sheram) was born in 1857 in Alexandropol (Leninakan). His grandfather was the ashugh Kyamili and his cousin was Mkrtich Talyan - the ashugh Jamali. The latter was married to Jivani, a young ashugh who had just arrived from Akhalkalaki province. Sheram's and Jamali's fathers, Karapet and Hovhannes Talyan's, were brothers. They ran a large cafe in the city since the 1860s, called Ghaifa. It was the central gathering place for all local master ashughs and music performances took place almost every evening. Grigor listened to the ashughs a lot in his childhood and was impressed. At the age of ten, due to the death of his father, he left his primary education, entered a carpenter's workshop and practiced carpentry until he was twenty-two years old. In 1872, he set the hatchet aside and took up the tar that he had made for himself.

However, Grigor did not follow the path of Jivani and Jamali. That is, he did not become an ashugh in the traditional sense of the word. Instead, he became a singer-instrumentalist and the author of love poems, who did not participate in the performances of professional ashughs, competitions, or cafe life. He formed his own musical ensemble with his friends playing chianur[3] and cymbals and started performing at public and family gatherings and parties. Grigor Talyan with his lively, emotional songs and masterful playing or "Usta Gokor, known by the citizens, gradually created fame around his name, and became a favorite in regions outside his city. He and his ensemble were invited to city clubs to regularly perform at parties and to give artistic pleasure to a music-loving population. He was invited to Kars, Etchmiadzin, Yerevan to perform at public parties and make his song and music heard.

In 1913, Talyan went to Astrakhan, Russia after being invited to take part in a festive party organized on the occasion of the 1500th anniversary of the invention of the Armenian alphabet.

In 1914, the Armenian Cultural Society organized a big ethnographic party in Baku. Grigor Talyan, who was invited to take part in that party, performed his song and music, leaving a great impression on the listeners. Poet Hovhannes Hovhannisyan, hearing the master perform his "smooth-like-silk" songs, called him "Ashugh Sheram[4]".

In 1916, our master moved to Tbilisi (Georgia), where he was warmly welcomed by the people of Alexandropol origin and the Armenian music lovers in general. In 1922, on the occasion of the 35th anniversary of his activity, a literary-artistic party was organized, where the ashough himself performed his latest songs, others spoke with a word of respect, and the author's poems were read. In 1926, Sheram returned to his hometown of Leninakan, where the 40th anniversary of his activity was solemnly celebrated, with the participation of a choir, an orchestra, and a troupe of ashough singers and artists.

---

[3] Eastern string musical instrument.

[4] Sheram in Armenian means silkworm.

In 1935, our master took his beloved and inseparable tar and moved to Yerevan to settle in the capital of Armenia forever. Despite his respectable 78-year-old height, he seemed to have not lost his energy and vivacity to continue his singing and music. He was granted a pension by the Armenian government, then he became a member of the Soviet Writers' Union. The Radio Committee of Armenia very often translated Sheram's songs, communicating them to the entire population of Armenia. However the master's physique was not up to par with his mental strength. He was diagnosed with incurable cancer and died on July 3, 1938 at the age of 81.

THE LITERARY HERITAGE OF SHERAM

Sheram has written several hundred verses. Many of these verses or songs have been published in the past in the following booklets.

A. "K'nar" ("Քնար") - by singer Grigor Talyan. Adapted to his composed and Eastern melodies. Published in Alexandropol, 1902, 74 pages.

B. "Gangati shanter" ("Գանգատի շանթեր") - published as a separate booklet in 1905, which includes revolutionary and patriotic songs. The book is published under the "Petrograd" nickname.

C. "Ser ev kriv" ("Սեր և կռիվ") - Grigor Talyan, Alexandropol, 1907, 112 pages. Songs of love and struggle. Printed on the cover of the booklet is the following.

> *Go nightingale, fly away*
> *Away from this bloody world,*
> *Go nightingale, don't stay here,*
> *Separated from your rose.*

D. "Waterless Garden" - Grigor Talyan, Alexandropol, 1913, 94 pages. Printed on the cover is the following.

I've planted a rose,
But harvested a heartache,
I've searched for a love,
But found only wounds.

E. "Unrestrained race" - Grigor Talyan, Alexandropol, 1915, 32 pages. Printed on the cover.

This terrible labor,
Must give birth to a new life,
Desirable bright future,
Requires big redemption.

The heirs of the ashough have many atypical songs, collected in a notebook, written by the author's youngest son, Vazgen Talyan.

THE THEME OF SHERAM'S SONGS

Sheram songs are mainly about love. He is a love singer first and foremost. In the current collection, as the reader will see, 62 out of 80 songs are love songs and his best melodies are composed for those songs. But Sheram's love, as it becomes clear, was everlasting and unattainable. His youthful love remained until his old age. He was inspired by it; he could not compose and sing without having an image of it in front of his eyes.

You are my muse,
I cannot sing
Without you.
The harp of my heart
No one can tune.
Except for you.

Or,

With tar in my hands, day and night,
I sing for you,
There are many beautiful pigeons in this garden,
But, my quail, I dream only of you ...

Sheram has always been surrounded by beauties. His song, music, and charming lines captivated other women, but he always remained faithful to his love, composing these lines,

Beauties, do not be offended,
If I always praise my beloved,
You will not know my sorrow,
That's why I praise my love,
That's why I praise my angel.

Sheram has very beautiful completely independent lines in his love songs. He sings simple, almost colloquial language, but with beautiful images.

You walk like a gazelle,
Running away from the hunter,
You give life to the one who sees you,
You are taken wild from the forest.

Tell me, who are you looking for,
With your eyes shining bright,
Who is your master? Who do you love,
You, the apple of Paradise.

After love songs, Sheram's next main literary theme is dedicated to the struggle, patriotic, sad past, of which only a few are included in this collection. There are few public, everyday songs dedicated to the evil of the day, the publication of which remains for the future.

We gave the last place to the satirical poems, of which only five were at the disposal of the editorial office.

LANGUAGE OF THE SONGS

The language of Sheram's songs cannot be said to be dialectal. He is essentially literary, but words from the Alexandropol dialect are widely used, a city where the use of Turkish words in Sheram's adolescent's and youth life was very common in colloquial language. For example, յամդուն, յորդան, դուշ, վախտ, սերրան, դուշման and many other similar words. The citizens of Alexandrapol did not even realize that these were foreign words and that we have those words in Armenian.

In the present case, we did not consider it our right to proofread the language of our author, but left it as he wrote it[5].

Sheram has invented several self-created words, as well, for example, չրբանել - to walk kneeling. սազատար - a person who withstands the coquetry of someone. In some cases, the author has also abbreviated spelling of some words or etymological deviations, involuntarily sacrificing the purity of the language to the rhymes.

POETRY

Ashugh Sheram did not weave his songs according to the rules of melody traditionally accepted in the ashugh literature, as other ashughs did by using their *ghoshmans, divans, ghazals, mukhambaz,*

---

[5] The current editorial team has put together a comprehensive dictionary of these terms at the end of this book to help the reader to navigate Sheram's poetry with ease.

etc[6]. Our author did not follow the complex and diverse poetic structures of the ashugh style from the beginning. He not only he kept himself away from all of them, but he also did not need those structures and their melodies, because he composed his own melodies and adjusted his own verses to those melodies according to his own poetic verse structures. For example, in the same song, we come across lines that have one syllable more or less compared to the other lines because the melody demands it. In such cases, the author sacrificed the rules adopted in the versification in favor of the melody.

Sheram loves the verse structure called folk bayati. As it is known, all the "Jangyulums" (folk quatrains) are composed in that way: that is, four lines of seven syllables each, of which the lines 1st, 2nd, and 4th are identical, for example,

Folk

Հանդում բուսել է **unկոն**,
Մերդ թխել է **բոքոն**,
Մեռնիմ ծոցիդ նռներին,
Կըլմանի վարդի **կոկոն:**

*Handum bousel e **sokon**,*
*Meryd t'khel e **bok'on**,*
Mernim tsots'id nyrnerin,
*Kylmani vardi **kokon**.*

Hovhannes Hovhannisyan

Ալագյազ բարձր **սարին**
Ձյուն ա կիտել **կատարին**,
Սարի չամբեք' բաց էլեք՝
Էրթամ հասնիմ իմ **յարին:**

*Alagyaz bardzr **sarin**,*
*Dzyun a kitel **katarin**,*
Sari chambek' bats' elek',
*Ert'am hasnim im **yarin**.*

---

[6] Ghoshmans, divans, ghazals, mukhambaz, are some of the ashugh poetry genres and rhyme structures.

Sheram

Էլի երկինքս ամմել է,   Eli yerkinqk's **ampel e**,
Յարրս ալ ձին թամբել է,   Yarys al dzin **t'ambel e**,
Ըածեն խրրովել՝ կերթա,   Yndzen khyrrovel kert'a,
Բողշես կապել, ճամբել է: Boghches kapel, **tchambel e**.

Թարլան, թարլան իմ յարր,   T'arr'lan, t'arr'lan im **yary**,
Դարդերիս դեղ ու ճարր,   Darderis degh u **chary**,
Ծըլած ծաղկած հանդի մեջ,   Tsylats, tsaghkats handi mej,
Քնաց է իմ սարդարր: K'nats e im **sardary**.

This is the first time that we publish and make available to the general public the songs of Grigor Talyan - Ashugh Sheram with their melodies, the songs that are already popular among music loving audience.

Garegin Levonyan
Honored Art Worker

SONG LYRICS

You Are My Muse

My muse,
I have no voice
Without you.
My heart's harp strings
Play out of tune
Except for you.

> *Oh, lovely lady,*
> *Your eyes, your rosy cheeks,*
> *Your luscious hair and brow,*
> *No rouge can enrich*
> *My heavenly angel.*

Without you
It hurts to stay,
Or live alone.
Please let me die
Or give me life
My love, my lady.

Trinkets, decorations:
You do not need them,
You have a dove's beauty.
Red henna dresses your body,
Like sweet marzipan
You are, my love

Your youth betrays you,
Just bloomed
As a spring bouquet.
I give myself to you,
Don't you understand?
You heartless one.

Դու իմ մուսան ես

Դու իմ մուսան ես,
Առանց քեզի
Երգել չեմ կարող.
Սրտիս տավիղը
Բացի քեզնից
Էլ չունիմ լարող։

> *Սիրուն, սև աչերուդ, կարմիր վարդ այտերուդ,*
> *Շուխ մազերուդ, շանթ ունքերուդ*
> *Էլ ինչ սուրմա է հարկավոր*
> *Էդ աննման փերուդ։*

Քեզանից հեռու
Դառն է մնալ,
Ապրել միայնակ,
Կուզես սպանի,
Կուզես կյանք տուր,
Սիրուն աղավնյակ։

Ջարդ ու զարդարանք
Էլ ինչ պետք է,
Դու սիրուն դուշ ես,
Մարմինդ է զուգված
Ալ խալերով,
Դրախտի նուշ ես։

Ափսոս ջահել ես,
Նոր ես ծաղկել
Փնջիկդ զարնան,
Քեզ ջան եմ տալիս՝
Չես հասկանում,
Անգութ հոգեհան։

Oh, Deep Vast Seas

Oh, deep vast seas, calm down please
Your raging waves that storm,
My heart, aflame, blows in the breeze
I've lost my way home.

      I cared for her like a velvet rose,
      And cherished softly day by day
      Caressed her chest…
      Her coyness gave me a bolt,
      And her golden hair
      Set my heart arrest,
      My love, my love, my love!

I've lost my love,
So let me go in pain
To find the blissful one
And fall into her arms again.

I begged the mountains
Without end, but I am scorned.
Crying on my knees, they yielded
But promises were torn.

I beg once more,
Please help me find my dove!
My heart is softened, uncalloused
It's thirsty for her love.

Խոր, մեծ ծովեր

Խոր մեծ ծովեր, մեղմացուցեք
Ալիքները ձեր կատաղած,
Վառված սրտիս հով սփռեցեք
Անդեկ նավ եմ անճար թողած։

> *Խաս վարդի պես պահեցի,*
> *Նուշ-անուշ փայփայեցի,*
> *Քաքույշ լանջր շոյեցի,*
> *Սրտադող նազերը,*
> *Ուկեշող մազերը.*
> *Մի գերի են շինել ինձ,*
> *Յա՛ր, յա՛ր, յա՛ր։*

Կորուցել եմ հոգուս յարին,
Թողեք անցնիմ բալքի գտնիմ
Մուրազատու իմ սարդարին,
Սիրտս առնիմ գիրկը ընկնիմ։

Սարերին շատ աղաչեցի,
Շատ խնդրեցի, բայց մերժեցին,
Նրանց փեշին ծունկ չոքեցի,
Խոստացան տալ, բայց դրժեցին։

Այժմ եկել ձեզ կաղաչեմ,
Ճամփա կուզեմ՝ էրթամ յարիս,
Սիրահար եմ, կարծր քար չեմ,
Շատ եմ ծարավ հոգետարիս։

Beautiful Peacock

You came and stood before me,
Taking my heart away,
Adorned in red and green,
Like a peacock, my pixie.

> *My love, my beauty, my sun,*
> *Your smile is like a rose*
> *Your cheerful look*
> *I yearn for*
> *My sweet, my graceful one.*

Your eyes glimmer in the night
Your lips are melon red
Your dazzling eyebrows bewitch my heart
Your bosom a revelation.

Please depart, blind me from
Your presence and your gaze
Perhaps one day I'll be lucky
And kiss your cheeks ablaze.

Սիրուն սիրամարգ

Եկել ես կանգնել աչքիս առաջ,
Ձիգյարս քյաբաբ ես արել,
Հագել ես կերպաս ալ ու կանաչ,
Սիրուն սիրամարգ ես դառել։

      Արևիդ մատաղ, բարևիդ մատաղ,
      Նազելի յար,
      Գեղեցիկ վարդ ես, դեմքով զվարթ ես
      Սիրուն, կարոտ եմ քեզ, կարոտ,
      Ա՛խ, ազիզ, անուշ, աննման յար։

Աստղերից պայծառ աչքեր ունես,
Շրթունքդ նռան կեղև են,
Ներերից շանթող ունքեր ունես,
Ծծերդ լույս են, արև են։

Հեռացիր, գռնե էլ չտեսնեմ,
Չինարի բոյդ, պատկերդ։
Մուրազիս բալքի մեկ օր հասնեմ,
Համբուրեմ շառաղ այտերդ։

Dear, Dear, My Dearest Love

You sing so softly, sweetly,
Dear, dear, my dearest love,
You step with swiftness and grace
Dear, dear, my dearest love,

> *Your beautiful eyes and brows,*
> *Sona love, Sona love,*
> *Bewilder those who see you,*
> *Your almond eyes and arched brows,*
> *As a gazelle, gazelle, gazelle…*

How elegant is your beauty
Dear, dear, my dearest love.
What kindles the fire in your heart
Dear, dear, my dearest love.

Oh, graceful lady, please let me know,
Dear, dear, my dearest love,
Who is your beloved?
Dear, dear, my dearest love.

Ջա՛ն, ջա՛նիդ դուռբան

Խոսում ես մեղմիկ, անուշ,
Ջա՛ն, ջա՛ն, ջա՛ն, ջանիդ դուռբան,
Քայլերդ համեստ, զգույշ.
Ջա՛ն, ջա՛ն, ջա՛ն, ջանիդ դուռբան։

> Սիրուն աչքեր, ունքերդ,
> Սո՛նա յար, Սո՛նա յար,
> Տեսնողիդ կանես ապուշ,
> Խաժուժ աչքեր, կամար ունքեր,
> Ջեյրա՛ն, ջեյրա՛ն, ջեյրա՛ն...

Որքան կոկլիկ, սիրուն ես,
Ջա՛ն, ջա՛ն, ջա՛ն, ջանիդ դուռբան,
Աճապ սրտիդ սեր ունե՞ս,
Ջա՛ն, ջա՛ն, ջա՛ն, ջանիդ դուռբան։

Եկ ինձ ասա, նազ աղջիկ,
Ջա՛ն, ջա՛ն, ջա՛ն, ջանիդ դուռբան,
Աճապ մեկին սիրու՞մ ես,
Ջա՛ն, ջա՛ն, ջա՛ն, ջանիդ դուռբան։

You Went To Araz Today

You went to Araz today,
Bathing, you became a fairy,
Your light casts a shadow over darkness,
Like an immortal angel.

> *You are sweetness,*
> *Your words sweet*
> *Your breath sweet*
> *I kissed your lips*
> *And tasted the sweetest sweetness.*

With soft pink satin
Caressing your neck like kisses
You are stunning and shining
Like the spring sun.

I have no pen or eloquent tongue
To put your praise into words.
You shock all who see you
Like the lightning of a summer storm.

---

* *Araz is the name of Araks river.*

Էսօր Արազն ես գնացել

Էսօր Արազն ես գնացել,
Լողացել՝ փերի ես դարձել,
Խավարին շավաղ ես գցել,
Անման հրեշտակի նման։

> *Իփքրդ անուշ, խոսքրդ անուշ, շունչրդ անուշ,*
> *Շրթունքներդ համբուրեցի՝ զգացի ամենքից անուշ։*

Հագել ես վարդագույն ատլաս,
Փաթաթել վզիդ ալ ու խասա,
Պճնվել ես, կշողշողաս,
Գարնան արեգակի նման։

Չունիմ գրիչ, լեզու ճարտար,
Գրեմ, գովեմ անձիդ համար,
Դիտողիդ կանես շանթահար,
Ամառվա կայծակի նման։

I Love You

I love you, but you don't see it.
You broke my heart
Because you're heartless
My blossoming chinaberry.

You put the pitcher upon your shoulder
On your way to the spring, through the flower fields.
Please take my golden bowl with you,
And bring me some water as well.

Please come back and let me see
Your fiery eagle's eyes.
And if I cannot quench that thirst
Send me a kiss from afar.

Every night I make a vow
To that fresh and sweet spring,
I will always drink her waters
Where my love has stirred.

Սիրում եմ քեզ

Սիրում եմ քեզ՝ խաբար չունիս,
Խորովել ես ջիգյարս,
Դու հեչ սիրտ ու ջիգյար չունիս,
Փունջ-փունջ ծաղկած չինարս։

Կուժը ուսիդ աղբյուր կերթաս,
Ծաղկոտ դաշտի վրայով,
Առ, քեզ հետ տար իմ ոսկե թաս,
Ջուրմ էլ ինձ բեր քո ձեռքով։

Կամ թե մեկ ետ դարձիր՝ տեսնեմ
Արծվի յանդուն աչերդ,
Մուրազիս էլ որ չհասնեմ,
Հեռվից խլեմ պաչերդ։

Ամեն գիշեր ուխտ եմ գնում
Էն պարզ, անուշ աղբյուրին,
Որտեղից միշտ ջուր եմ խմում,
Սերըս խառնեմ էն ջրին։

I Am The One, Stunned

I loved her, she stole my thoughts,
Deceived me, stole my sanity.
I thought she was my love,
But she stole my loving heart.

> *Dark stars,*
> *Wild birds*
> *Like you,*
> *I am the one, stunned.*

I was sweet but have turned bitter.
I was a master but am now a servant.
My heartless love has tortured me,
Blinded by my heart and soul.

Muddy rivers, please dry,
Make way for Sheram.
My love is lost in this darkness,
You cry the sorrow of my heart.

Մէկն էլ ես եմ շվարած

Սիրեցի, խելքս տարավ,
Մոլորեց՝ միտքս տարավ,
Նրան յար էի կարծել,
Սիրամոլ սիրտս տարավ։

    Խավար ապրդեր,
    Անրուն հավքեր,
    Ձեզի նման
    Մէկն էլ ես եմ շվարած։

Անուշ էի՝ դառնացա,
Տեր էի՝ ծառա դարձա,
Անսիրտ յարս ինձ ատեց,
Հոգով, սրտով կուրացա։

Պղտոր գետեր չորացեք,
Շերամիս ճամփա բացեք,
Սերս մթան մեջ կորավ,
Դուք սրտիս դարդը լացեք։

That's My Love

Who has seen a pomegranate growing on a cypress?
Or a bright moon grafted in its leaves?

> *She can't be found in any garden,*
> *She was never born in this world,*
> *She is my master,*
> *She is my love,*
> *She is my fairy,*
> *I'm heartbroken,*
> *For I'm in love,*
> *I'm weakened,*
> *And remiss.*
> *Leave me be*
> *I am crestfallen.*

Who has seen the tiny stars in your eyes?
Whose lips pucker as flower petals?

That moon is the temple of my beloved
That cypress is my beloved's physique

That pair of pomegranates are wellsprings of life
Those scattered stars makes me foolish.

Են իմ սերն է

Ո՛վ է տեսել նոճի ծառին նուռ բուսած,
Տերևներում չքնաղ լուսնիկ պատրուսած:

> Ոչ մեկ պարտիզում դեռ չեմ տեսել,
> Ոչ էլ աշխարհում հազիվ է ծավել,
> Են իմ վերն է,
> Են իմ սերն է,
> Են իմ փերին է,
> Դարդոտ եմ...
> Ա՛խ, սովդաքյար եմ,
> Անդեղ ու ճար եմ,
> Անհոգատար եմ:
> Ասրված սիրողը, սիրտ ունեցողը,
> Թող չդիպնի՝ ես վշտահար եմ:

Ո՛վ է տեսել աչքերի տեղ աստղիկներ,
Ո՛վ է գձել շրթունքի տեղ ծաղիկներ:

Են լուսնիկը սիրուն յարիս ճակատն է,
Են ճնարին իմ թաղանիս հասակն է:

Են գույգ նուռը կաթնադբյուր են կենսական,
Վառ աստղիկներ լույս են շաղում հոգեհամ:

This Is My Sweetheart

This is my sweetheart,
She is a fire, an inferno, blazing flames,
She burned me, snared me,
And torched my heart into ashes.

Whoever can, let them approach
This fiery inferno.
Who is brave enough to endure
Such deep sorrowful wounds.

I bundled roses for my heartbreak,
Cupped the cornucopia in my palms,
Breathing in the fragrance,
It reeks of pain instead of roses.

Մի բալա է

Մի բալա է էս իմ յարրս,
Մի յանդուն է, հուր ու բոց.
Խանձեց-խորվեց, կտրեց ճարս,
Իմ ջիգյարս շինեց խոց:

Ով կարող է՝ թող մոտենա,
Էս յանդունին, էս բոցին,
Կտրիճ կուզեմ, որ դիմանա
Էսքան դարդին, խոր խոցին:

Դարդեր, վարդեր, մեկ եմ հյուսել,
Զեռքրս առել զարդի տեղ,
Ես ուզում եմ փունջ հոտոտել,
Դարդ եմ շչում վարդի տեղ:

Like Rose Buds

Like budding roses
You'll open one day
For you, countless nightingales
Will cry day and night.

You shine like the sun
Setting hearts on fire,
Whomever loves you wholeheartedly
Will feel the heat of your flame.

Two celestial stars
Shine upon your face,
Beneath the bow of your brow,
Striking my heart with a bolt.

Կոկոն վարդերի նման

Կոկոն վարդերի նման
Բացվում ես դու անպայման,
Քեզ համար շատ սոխակներ
Գիշեր ցերեկ կչողբան:

Արևի պես փայլում ես,
Մատաղ սրտեր այրում ես,
Ով քեզ սրտով է սիրում,
Նրան էլ տոչորում ես:

Երկու աստղեր երկնային,
Ցոլում են քո լույս դեմքին,
Ադեղ ունքերիդ տակին,
Շանթահարում իմ սրտին:

You Are Divine

You are divine, you are love and wonder
I long for the fire in your eyes
You have me on my knees, captured, heart alight,
Speak, so I may know your voice.

> *When the nightingale sees you,*
> *It will sing its wishes true,*
> *Flying beside you always,*
> *It won't languish anymore.*

I have picked wildflowers from the mountains and valleys,
Plucked them delicately,
Bundled the bouquet at their stems,
I came to your door and fell at your feet.

I have nothing else to give you as a gift,
Trust in my devotion, do not make me beg,
Take this bouquet and set my heart on fire,
I will open the closed doors of love again.

Սիրուն ես, հոգյակ

Սիրուն ես, հոգյակ, սեր ես ու սիրուն,
Մատաղ եմ կտրել քո լույս աչերուն,
Էրված ու գերված չոքել կսպասեմ,
Մեկ անգամ խոսիր՝ էդ լեզուդ լսեմ:

Բլբուլը երբ քեզի վեանի,
Իր փափագին պիտի-պիտի հասնի,
Թե որ լինի միշտ քեզի մոտ,
Էլ չի քաշի քեզի կարոտ:

Սարեն ու ձորեն ծաղկունք եմ ջոկել,
Քսքուշ ու ընտիր շըթունքով պռկել,
Վատվռուն ակունք մեկ տեղ փունջ կապել,
Եկել եմ դողդ, փեշդ եմ ընկել:

Ուրիշ բան չունիմ քեզ նվեր տալու,
Ընդունիր ձոնս, մի թողնի լալու,
Դե'հ, առ մուրազ տուր, վեր կենամ գնամ,
Սիրային փակված դռներ ետ բանամ:

37

It's A Cool Night

It's a cool night. Come out. The moon is new,
Sweet girl, your love has set my mind astray,
Tall as a sycamore, I am taken breathless,
Sweet love, come soon, tender love, come soon.

> *Your towering beauty sends my heart skyward*
> *Gazelle, gazelle, gazelle,*
> *Your silken braid twists my heart askew*
> *Gazelle, gazelle, gazelle.*

Stars glow in the clear sky,
Brightening my heart with your dark gaze,
I've lost myself, I weep in your palms,
Sweet love, come soon, tender love, come soon.

It would be a shame to walk this night alone,
I beg, but you won't emerge. How can I go on without you?
If you want my soul, my dear, my sweetheart, it is yours.
Sweet love, come soon, tender love, come soon.

Ցուլ գիշեր է

Ցուլ գիշեր է, դուրս եկ, լուսնյակը նորել է,
Նուշ աղջիկ, քո սիրուց հանգիստս կորել է,
Էղ չինար հասակդ իմ խելքը տարել է,
Անուշ յա՛ր, շուտ արի, քնքույշ յա՛ր, շուտ արի։

Բոյ ու բուսիդ մատաղ,
Ջեյրան, ջեյրան, ջեյրան,
Մեղաքս հուսիդ մատաղ,
Ջեյրան, ջեյրան, ջեյրան։

Աստղեր կշողշողան պարզորակ երկնքեն,
Վառեցիր իմ հոգին քո սև-սև աչերեն,
Համբերանքս կտրավ, լալիս եմ քո ձեռքեն...
Անուշ յա՛ր, շուտ արի, քնքույշ յա՛ր, շուտ արի։

Ափսոս էս գիշերին, որ մենակ ման կուգամ,
Կաղաչեմ, դուրս չես գա, առանց քեզ ու՞ր գնամ,
Թե հոգիս էլ ուզես, ազիզ ջան, քեզ կուտամ,
Անուշ յա՛ր, շուտ արի, քնքույշ յա՛ր, շուտ արի։

My Gazelle, Come Gently

Every evening, every morning,
I wait for you, my love, with hunger and thirst,
Heavenly angel, why deprive me,
And leave my heart aching?

> *My dear, come gently,*
> *Take pause,*
> *My love is devoted,*
> *Let's not waste a breath.*

I'm hopelessly lost looking for you,
My heart longs for your radiance,
Only you can
Feed my starving heart

How did you become so cold?
You've abandoned Sheram, my love
You do not even visit in my dreams,
You've killed that voice and forgotten me.

Մարալ ջան, հեգ արի

Ամեն երեկո, ամեն առավոտ,
Շամփեդ կսպասեմ, յա՛ր, պապակ ու կարոտ,
Աննման փերի, ինչու՞ գրկեցիր,
Թողիր ինձ այսպես չիգյարս յարոտ։

    Մարալ ջա՛ն, հեգ արի,
    Քիչ-քիչմ թեգ արի,
    Ընձեն լավ յար չունիս,
    Հեչ-հեչ մի՛ թեգարի։

Մոլոր ու շվար քեզ եմ որոնում,
Սիրտս է անվերջ, յա՛ր, լույս մարմնիդ տենչում,
Բացի քեզանից ոչ ոք չի կարող
Մտնել էս պապակ չիգյարիս խորքում։

Ինչու՞ց էր այդպես ապառաժ դարձար,
Շերամիս ընկած, յա՛ր, թողիր հեռացար,
Գոնե երազով էլ ինձ չես գալիս,
Խիղճդ մեռուցիր, իսպառ մոռացար։

You Are A Red Winged Dove

I have always loved you and given you my soul,
Your sweet words have stolen my thoughts,
Bring me to life, don't let me despair,
You've pierced my heart with your love.

> *My dear, you are sweet,*
> *You are the royal flower of my garden,*
> *You're a red winged dove,*
> *More tender than a rose.*

I am your love, the trinket of your touch,
Be careful not to cut the strings of my lyre,
Make me yours, for I have found sorrow,
Do not lead my captive heart astray.

I would rather be put to death,
Than to separate myself from you,
You have a good heart, I'm not fooled,
Come close to me just once.

Ալդանաղ դուշ ես

Միշտ քեզ եմ սիրել, հոգիս նվիրել,
Էդ անուշ լեզուդ խելքըս է տարել.
Արի ինձ կյանք տուր, մի թողնի տխուր,
Սիրտս ես խարել 'էշխիդ նետը սուր:

Ազիզ, անուշ ես,
Խաս բաղի նուշ ես,
Ալդանաղ դուշ ես,
Վարդեն քքնուշ ես:

Ես եմ քո յարը, մատնունդ գոհարը,
Զգույշ՝ չկտրես քսարիս լարը,
Տար ինձ դոպ էրա, գտի մեկ չարա,
Քեզ գերի սիրտս մի թողնի յարա:

Իրավունք կուտամ, որ ինձ սպանես,
Քան թե բաց աչքով քեզնից բաժանես.
Սիրտ ունիս բարի, մի հնար ճարի,
Գոնե մեկ անգամ ինձ մոտիկ արի:

Look Back For Me Once

Like the sun you emerged out the door
And set the world on fire
You passed by gently,
Filling our hearts alight.

> *Filling my heart with endless sorrow,*
> *You turned your back and left,*
> *Casting me aside,*
> *Look back for me once,*
> *Just once, just once,*
> *For I am your love, I am your master,*
> *Don't let me die in vain.*

What a beautiful body you have decorated!
But nature already painted you,
Your eyes ignite,
Burning adolescent hearts.

Դարձի´ր մեկ աշեն

Արևը դիպավ, դռնեն դուրս էկար,
Բոլոր աշխարհը արիր շանթահար,
Դու նազ անելով անցար գնացիր,
Բյուրավոր սրտեր կրակով լցրիր։

Սիրտս լցրիր բյուր ցավերով,
Ու հեռացել կերթաս,
Ինձ մոռացել կերթաս,
Դարձի´ր մեկ աշեն, մեկ աշեն, մեկ աշեն,
Կայսի մեկ աշեն, մեկ աշեն, մեկ աշեն,
Քո սերն եմ, քո փերն եմ, զուր չենենեմ։

Էդ չքնաղ մարմնիդ էլ ի՞նչ զարդարվել,
Երբ բնությունն է քեզի նկարել,
Էդ սև աչերդ կրակ կցայտեն,
Շատ մատաղ սրտեր կայրեն-խորովեն։

45

I Beg You Mountains

Mountains, please, abate,
I'm going to my love, give way,
For God's sake, don't close my path,
I am thirsting, my heart is a whirl.

Like a fallen leaf upon your slope,
I have lain hopeless all season,
Let me pass and reach my beloved,
If I see her, I'll not die of longing.

Longing, oh the longing, how my heart aches,
The way is treacherous and sharp
I loved her from a young age,
But devils took her away.

They took her away, and my sun turned black,
Bringing my world to ruin,
I live, but I am numb,
I do not have love for anyone else.

Sheram, your beloved's heart is frozen,
Why did you become a fire butterfly in vain?
Why are you begging the mountains and the stone,
When someone else owns your beloved?

Սարեր կաղաչեմ

Սարեր, կաղաչեմ, իջեք ցածրացեք,
Գնում եմ յարիս, մի ճամփա բացեք,
Աստված կրսիրեք ճամփես մի՛ք կապի՝
Շատ եմ պապակել, սիրտս կշտապի։

Ձեր փեշին թոշնած տերևի նման,
Ընկած եմ վաղուց անհույս, անգյուման,
Թույլ տվեք անցնիմ էրթամ յարիս մոտ,
Բալքի մեկ տեսնիմ՝ չմեռնիմ կարոտ։

Կարոտ, ա՛խ, կարոտ, ջիգյարս յարոտ,
Հե՛յ ճամփես չաթին, փշոտ է քարոտ,
Ջահել հասակից սիրեցի նրան,
Բայց նամարդ մարդիկ խլեցին տարան։

Խլեցին տարան, արևս սևցավ,
Բաժին աշխարհրս վերանա դարձավ,
Ապրում եմ, համա ապրումներ չունիմ,
Էլ ուրիշ մեկին սեր-սավդա չունիմ։

Շերամ, սեզ յարիդ սիրտոըն է ստել,
Էլ ի՛նչ ես իզուր փարվանա դառել,
Զոքել կաղաչես սարին ու քարին,
Ուրիշն է տիրել քո սիրած յարին։

I Became Lost

A beautiful thing transpired one day,
From where did she descend?
She vanquished me without a sword, roasted without flame,
Exposing my heart and soul.

> *I became lost,*
> *I shed tears of blood,*
> *I glimpsed the vision of an angel,*
> *But, alas, I lost her!*

She pierced my heart with sharp arrows unknowingly,
From that day on my light diminished,
Where should I search? Where would she be found?
Let her bury me with her own hands.

I do not know if she flew into the air,
An angel soaring back to heaven,
Maybe I saw her in my dreams,
Where she promised a heartfelt love.

Ոլոր-մոլոր

Մի գեղեցիկ պատահեցավ ինձ հանկարծ,
Չհասկացա ինչ ցեղից էր նա ծնված,
Անսուր մործեց, առանց կրակ խորովեց ինձ,
Խաղաղ սիրտս ու հոգիս արավ խոցալից։

    Ոլոր-մոլոր մասցի,
    Արյուն արցունք թափեցի,
    Այսպես մի հրեշտակ տեսա,
    Բայց, ավա՜ղ շուտ զրկվեցա։

Սուր-սուր նետեր սիրտս խրեց ու անցավ,
Հենց այն օրից լույս արևս խավարավ,
Էլ ու՞ր փնտրեմ, ո՞րտեղ գտնեմ ես նրան,
Որ իր ձեռքով նա ինձ դնե գերեզման։

Չգիտեմ, թե նա օղի մեջ սլացավ,
Թե հրեշտակ էր դեպի երկինք վերացավ,
Գուցե տեսա երազիս մեջ ես նրան,
Որ խոստացավ լինել սրտով սիրեկան։

My Sky Is Cloudy Again

My sky is gloomy again,
My love has saddled the red horse,
Upset with me, she flees,
Packed her things and set off.

> *Colourful birds, sweet breeze, beautiful world,*
> *Put my love at ease.*

There is no sun for me,
I cannot sleep,
I call for her, but she is gone,
My charm has waned.

I loved her with all my heart,
At long last I prevailed,
Silence yourself, oh foes!
Finding her took ages, losing her took a second.

My sweet day has bittered,
What have I done to be forgotten?
She shut the door on me,
And bolted.

She broke our bond,
Her love has frozen,
She shattered my heart and left,
It seems her heart is empty.

> *Masis, let me die upon your foothills,*
> *Give way to the emerald dove,*
> *My love took it, taking flight,*
> *Burnt my heart, taking flight.*

Էլի երկինքս ամպել է

Էլի երկինքս ամպել է,
Յարրս ալ ճին թամբել է,
Ընծեն խոսովել՝ կերթաս,
Բոխտես կապել՝ ճամփել է։

> Նախշուն հավքեր, անուշ հովեր, շեն աշխարհի,
> Ամեք յարիս հերիք զարկե քարեքար։

Արև չկա ինձ համար,
Չունիմ հանգիստ ու դադար,
Կանչեմ-կանչեմ չի գալիս,
Սերրս մնաց կիսկատար։

Հոգով, սրտով սիրեցի,
Անջատ-անջատ տիրեցի,
Լեզուդ լովի, հե՜յ, դուշման,
Ուշ գտա, շուտ կորուցի։

Անուշ օրս դառնացավ,
Մեղքս ի՞նչ էր՝ մոռացավ,
Դուռը վրրես փակ թողեց,
Հե՜յ վախ, գնաց հեռացավ։

Տրված խոսքեն դառել է,
Սրտի սերը սառել է,
Սիրտս պոկեց ու գնաց,
Կարծես սիրոտը մեռել է։

> Մասիս, մեռնիմ էդ քու փեշին,
> Ճամփա փուր զբրուխտ դշին,
> Յարս վեր առել՝ կերթա,
> Զիգյարս վառել՝ կերթա։

My Heart Still Cries Today

My heart still cries today
It has not seen its beloved,
The dark clouds return,
Fogging upon my head.

> *I wish she was thirsty,*
> *And I, a cold spring,*
> *I'd give her water,*
> *So she would give me a kiss.*

It seems my rose has withered,
No nightingales sing anymore,
It seems my luck has dried,
No flowers bloom anymore.

> *I wish she was a nightingale,*
> *And I, a rose garden,*
> *Day and night*
> *She would sing in my arms.*

Winds descended from the mountains,
Destroying my garden,
Destined to long for my love forever,
It was written upon my forehead.

> *I wish she was a swan,*
> *And I, a clean sea.*
> *She would swim in my bosom,*
> *With her whole body.*

Էլի էսօր սիրտս կուլա

Էլի էսօր սիրտս կուլա,
Սիրած յարին չի տեսել,
Էլի ամպեր քուլա-քուլա
Գլխիս դուման են դիզել:

> Նա լիներ ծառավ, իսկ ես՝ պաղ աղբյուր,
> Ջուր փայի նրան, նա ինձ՝ մեկ համբույր:

Կարծես վարդս թոռմած լինի,
Երգող բլբուլ էլ չունիմ,
Կարծես բախտս քնած լինի,
Սիրուն ամբուլ էլ չունիմ:

> Նա լիներ բլբուլ, ես՝ վարդուր պարտեզ,
> Գիշեր ու ցերեկ երգեր իմ գրկես:

Հողմեր իջան սարեն-քարեն,
Բադ ու բադչես ավրեցին,
Ընդմիշտ կարոտ մնալ յարեն,
Ճակտիս էսպես գրեցին:

> Նա լիներ կարապ, իսկ ես՝ մաքուր ծով,
> Միշտ իմ ծոցիս մեջ լողար ողջ մարմնով:

Beauties

Beauties, do not be offended,
If I always praise my beloved,
You will not know my sorrow,
That's why I praise my love,
That's why I praise my angel.

Even if you were doves
With wings wide open,
Flying up to the sky,
Again, I praise my love,
Again, I praise my angel.

No matter how much you bejewel yourselves,
Even if my love dresses in humble black, and you in florid red,
Again, I praise my love,
Again, I praise my angel.

Even if you become a peacock
With your ornate feathers,
Or a sweet singing nightingale,
Again, I praise my love,
Again, I praise my angel.

Your hair is woven gold,
Your eyebrows a crescent moon,
Your eyes are shining stars,
Again, I praise my love,
Again, I praise my angel,

Each one of you are angels,
That walk before me.
But you cannot captivate me,
That's why I praise my love,
That's why I praise my angel.

Սիրունները

Սիրուննե՛ր, միք նեղենա,
Որ միշտ իմ յարիս եմ գովում,
Դուք իմ դարդը չեք իմանա,
Էստի յարիս եմ գովում,
Էստի վերիս եմ գովում:

Թեկուզ լինիք աղավնյակ
Թնիկներդ լայն բաց արած,
Ճախրելով վեր բարձրանաք,
Էլի յարիս եմ գովում,
Էլի վերիս եմ գովում:

Որքան կուզեք զարդարվեք
Ալ ու եշիլ զուհարներով.
Յարս՝ սև, դուք՝ ալ հագեք,
Էլի յարիս եմ գովում,
Էլի վերիս եմ գովում:

Թեկուզ լինիք սիրամարգ
Ձեր նախշունիկ փետուրներով,
Կամ անուշ երգող սոխակ,
Էլի յարիս եմ գովում,
Էլի վերիս եմ գովում:

Մազերդ՝ ոսկե թելեր,
Ունքերդ՝ նորածին լուսին,
Աչքերդ՝ փայլուն աստղեր,
Էլի յարիս եմ գովում,
Էլի վերիս եմ գովում:

Ամենքդ մեկ-մեկ վերի
Աչքիս առաջ ման եք գալի,
Բայց ինձ չեք կարող գերի,
Էստի յարիս եմ գովում,
Էստի վերիս եմ գովում:

In The Garden Roses Bloom

In the garden, roses bloom
Waiting for their nightingales
Withering without their nightingales
Hoping to be wooed.

> *Who knocks on the door?*
> *Oh, my heart is shaking!*
> *Where does my love go?*
> *Ah, my heart is playing!*

River waves
Run fervent,
Wailing tears
From the eyes of a lover.

A love waits at home
Calling for her love,
Strumming her lyre,
Playing with woe.

The butterfly beside the light
Flutters non-stop
Beating from love
Unabated.

A love waits at home
Writing to her love
Longing for her love
As each passing day goes.

Պարիզում վարդեր բացված

Պարտիզում վարդեր բացված,
Կասպասեն սոխակի,
Առանց սոխակ թառամած,
Կարոտ են պսակի։

> *Արդյոք ով է, դուռն է թակում,*
> *Ա՜խ, սիրտս կողղա,*
> *Իմ սիրուհիս ու՞ր է գնում,*
> *Ա՜խ, սիրտս կտտաղա։*

Գետակի ալիքները
Գնում են խայտալով,
Սիրահարի աչերից
Արտասուք թափելով։

Սիրուհին տանը նստած
Սպասում է յարին,
Քնարը ձեռին բռնած
Նվագում լալագին։

Թիթեռը ծռագի մոտ
Շրջում է անդադար,
Մինչ իր վերջ սիրակարոտ
Զունի նա օր, դադար։

Սիրուհին տանը նստած
Գրում է նամակներ,
Խիստ տրտում կանցկացնե
Իր գեղեցիկ օրեր։

Your Beautiful Eyes

Spring beauty, sweet love
Come and cure my heartache,
It burns for you, for your love,
While you sit unaware.

> *Your eyes stun*
> *With aching, arching brows*
> *Sweetheart, my love*
> *Come, take me with you.*

I gave you my heart in vain,
Turned my bright days into darkness
Don't you see my heartache?
How it misses the sun!

I'll give you a gift, whatever your heart desires.
Do not forsake me,
I am sleepless, I am restless
Visit me just once.

I've left my rose,
I've resigned my work,
I've wasted my fortune,
To sing the songs of your bright love.

Աչքդ խումար

Գարուն, սիրուն, անուշ յար,
Արի, դարդիս արա ճար,
Ես քեզ համար էրվում եմ,
Դու նստել ես բեխաբար։

*Աչքդ խումար,
Ունքդ կամար,
Անուշիկ յա՛ր,
Արի փար։*

Իգուր սիրտս քեզ տվի,
Ալ օրս փոխվեց սևի,
Դարդես հեչ խաբար չունիս,
Թողիր կարոտ առնի։

Նվեր կուտամ, ի՞նչ կուզես,
Ինձ մի՛ թողնի սևերես,
Քուն չունիմ, դադար չունիմ,
Գոնե մեկ օր արի տես։

Վարդս թողի հեռացա,
Բան ու գործըս մոռացա,
Մալ ու մուլքս վատնեցի,
Վատ էշխեդ աշուղ դարձա։

She Is In The Mood

Sweet spring days have come,
Flowering valleys and fields overflowing
My love
Dressed in red.

> *She's in the mood,*
> *in the mood,*
> *in the mood*
> *She holds her saz in-hand,*
> *her saz in-hand,*
> *her saz in-hand,*
> *Strumming as she strolls,*
> *Stepping as a doe.*

A Skylark graced the field
A nightingale alighted upon a rose,
A thousand beauties, a thousand doctors,
The will never know my hearts sorrow.

The birds came in flocks,
My name is Ashugh Sheram,
I will call for you time and again,
Until I burn as Kyaram*.

---

* *Kyaram - hero of an eastern love epic "Asli and Kyaram" who was in love with beautiful Asli. Equivalent of Romeo from "Romeo and Juliet".*

Նա մի նազ ունի

Եկան գարնան անուշ օրեր,
Ծաղկով լցված դաշտեր, ձորեր,
Յարս գուզվել սեյրան կերթա,
Հազած-կասպած ալվան շորեր։

    Նա մի նազ ունի, նազ ունի, նազ ունի,
    Ձեռքին սազ ունի, սազ ունի, սազ ունի,
    Ջայլելով սեյրան կերթա,
    Դարձել է չեյրան՝ կերթա։

Արտուտն եկավ մտավ արտը,
Բլբուլն իջավ գրկեց վարդը,
Հազար սիրուն, հազար հեքիմ
Չեն իմանա սրտիս դարդը։

Հավքերն եկան երամ-երամ,
Անուն ունիմ աշուղ Շերամ,
Էսքան պիտի յարիս կանչեմ,
Տեյմոր վառվիմ որպես Քյարամ։

Beautiful, Beautiful

Beautiful, beautiful is my love,
A balm for all my pains
In the blossomed flower fields
My master sleeps.

> *My love is rare, my love is rare,*
> *There is none, there is none*
> *That shine like her among the stars,*
> *My love is rare, my love is rare,*
> *My love is a bird of paradise,*
> *I love you, my whim-bearer,*
> *I love you, my woe-bearer,*

I'll call upon her and court her heart,
I'll embrace her and take her home,
Embraced in her wonderous bosom
I'll open the love of my heart.

My heart's dearest,
The apple of my eye,
Flawless and pure,
A heavenly angel.

Թալյան, թալյան

Թալյան, թալյան իմ յարը,
Դարդերիս դեղ ու ճարը,
Ծլած-ծաղկած հանդի մեջ,
Քնած է իմ սարդարը։

> *Պալա՛ յարիս հայրը, ջանիս հայրը*
> *Չկա, չկա սաղ աշխարհի մեջ,*
> *Չկա վառ, պայծառ աստղերի մեջ,*
> *Յարիս հայրը, ջանիս հայրը, ջանիս հայրը։*
> *Դրախտի ծաղիկ է իմ յարը։*
> *Իմ նազապարին ես մատաղ,*
> *Իմ դարդապարին ես մատաղ։*

Էրթամ ձեն տամ, վեր հանեմ,
Վիզը ընկնիմ, տուն տանեմ,
Փաթաթվիմ անգին կրծքին,
Սրտիս սերը բաց անեմ։

Էս իմ սրտի սիրածին,
Էս իմ աչքի ջոկածին,
Հալալ-զուլալ ես մատաղ,
Աննման արարածին։

I've Sowed A Rose

Would you risk your hard heart
To come to my home?
Anguished by your love
Bring remedy with your love.

> *I've sowed a rose*
> *But harvested a heartache*
> *I've looked for love*
> *But discovered despair.*

My eyes grow weary in search of you,
Drop into my dreams if you please?
Grace me with your vision once more
Before this longing takes my heart.

If there are mountains you must pass
Borrow wings to fly past
If there are woes in your soul,
Wipe them out and be here soon.

My years go on rolling,
How quickly they transpire,
My heart goes on loving
This anguish still burns with desire.

Վարդ ցանեցի

Մեկ սիրտ էրաս, հե´յ անջիգյար.
Արի մեր տուն ներս մտի,
Ես հիվանդ եմ, յա´ր, քո դարդով,
Էդ քո սիրով ճար գտի:

> *Վարդ ցանեցի՝*
> *Դարդ քաղեցի,*
> *Յար փնտրեցի՝*
> *Յարա գտա:*

Աչքս մնաց, ա´խ, քո ճամփեդ,
Հեչ չէ արի երազով,
Մեկ էլ տեսնիմ շվա բոյդ,
Զեղնի մեռնիմ մուրազով:

Թե սարեր կան ճամփոդ վրա,
Թն ատ թռի, անց կացի,
Թե չարեր կան սրտիդ վրա,
Դուրս վոնդե, շուտ հասի:

Տարիներս գլոր-մլոր,
Ա´խ, շուտ անցան գնացին,
Իմ սավդալու սրտիս բոլոր,
Քու դարդերդ մնացին:

Cruel Judgement

Sweet girl sitting in this beautiful garden
Singing with a nightingale
Red roses, beautiful lilies, and gentle jasmines,
Hug your tender toes enchantedly.

> *My love, your silence*
> *Leaves my heart longing and*
> *Burning in flames.*
> *Tell me what I have done*
> *That you would be so cruel?*

How surprising that beneath your bosom,
So lush and luxurious, there is no fire and no love,
Though your angelic face glows virgin white
Your sweet song does not feed me.

Maybe you are a golden goddess,
Fallen from the heavens into this garden.
I've begged for your love a thousand times;
Instead of a kiss, you blacken my heart.

I ask a thousand questions, but you ignore me.
So, I will take my roaring heart and leave.
Mesmerized by your fiery eyes
I turn into a fool.

Անգույթ դապասպան

Ի՞նչ ես նստել գեղեցիկ բադի մեջ, ջան աղջիկ,
Սոխակի հետ ձայն ես բռնել ու երգում.
Կարմիր վարդն ու սիրուն շուշան, հեգ հասմիկ,
Հմայված փափուկ ոտքերդ են գրկում։

    Յա՜ր մեկ լուր չըվիր,
    Ծառավ ու պապակ թողիր,
    Ջիգյարս խորով արիր,
    Ի՞նչ մեղք ունիմ, որ դու այդպես
    Անգույթ դապասպան արիր։

Այդքան շբեղ, այդքան փարթամ կոծքի տակ,
Մի զարմանք է, որ կրակ ու սեր չկա,
Երեսդ լույս, գեղեցիկ կույս, հրեշտակ,
Քո անուշ երգից ինձ մագաչափի օգուտ չկա։

Միգուցե դու դիցուհի ես շողադեմ,
Դու շեկ ամպերից թոար իջար ես այգին,
Քեզ խնդրեցի հազար անգամ չոքած,
Համբույրի տեղ սրտիս դրիր սև կրակ։

Հազար հարցիս մեկ պատասխան չես տալիս,
Գոնե հանգիստ սիրտորս առնիմ հետանամ,
Ամեն անգամ հուր աչերիդ նայելիս,
Խելակորույս, անմիտք ապուշ կդառնամ։

My Lute On My Chest

With the lute on my chest, day and night,
I sing a song just for you,
Of all the birds that grace my garden,
Hail, my quail, I call for you.

> *Come, my dear!*
> *My ruby and coral,*
> *My shining jewel,*
> *My precious gem.*

How did I lose you?
Leaving, you won't return,
Perhaps you found a suitor more suited,
My love weeps for you.

Don't be heartless, just once,
Grace me with your face aglow,
Let me give you the last love in my heart,
My fragrant rose, my bird of paradise.

As long as there is breath within me
I cannot feel peace without you,
Despite the anguish you bestow my soul
I will not lament a moment.

Թառը դոշիս

Թառը դոշիս գօր ու գիշեր,
Սալթ քեզ համար խաղ եմ կանչում,
Բաղը շատ կան սիրուն ղռշեր,
Համա, լօրըս, քեզ եմ կանչում։

    Մեկ արի, յա՛ր ջան,
    Յաղութ ու մարջան,
    Շողշողուն քարըս,
    Անգին գոհարըս։

Ընչի էղպես հեռու ընկար,
Գնացիր, էլ ետ չես գալիս,
Վայ թե ընձեն լավը գտար...
Իմ սիրուն է քեզ համար լալիս։

Անսի՛րտ, հեչ չէ՞ թաք մեկ անգամ,
Արի տեսնիմ երեսդ լույս,
Մի սիրտ մնաց էն էլ քեզ տամ,
Հոտուն վարդս դրախտի բույս։

Քանի դեռ որ շունչ կա մեջըս,
Քեզնեն բնավ չեմ կշտանա,
Ինչքան էլ որ հոգիս տանջես,
Ոչ մի վայրկյան չեմ վշտանա։

I Wish It Was That Night

I wish it was that night,
When you promised me your love,
My golden bird, into your palms,
You took my aching heart away.

> *Ever since, I've become foolhardy,*
> *Anxious and uneasy with despair,*
> *You neither draw near,*
> *Nor truly depart.*

Your golden bowl is full of wine,
Sweet with the taste of desire,
Its destined for your chosen one,
Who will sleep dreaming of you.

I drank, and since that day
I've been drunk with your love,
If it was a promise, where is it?
Nothing else will quench my thirst.

Հազար էրնեկ

Հազար էրնեկ էն գիշերին,
Որ ինձ բույա տվեցիր,
Ուկե թոչսիկ, իմ հեզ սրտին,
Ձեռքդ զարկիր, խլեցիր:

    Էն օրվանեն բեխաբար,
    Եղա դադարկուն, անճար
    Ո՛չ մի անգամ մուրիկ կուգաս,
    Ո՛չ էլ խապար կհեռանաս:

Ուկե թասը լիքը գինով,
Անուշ գինով մուրազի,
Կտաս նրան հազար նազով,
Ով որ քեզ կըերազի:

Ես խմեցի... Էն օրվանեն
Դեռ հարբած եմ քո էշխեն,
Թե բույա էր, հապա ու՞ր է...
Չեմ հասնի իմ մուրազին:

Burning From Love

My starving heart burns for your love
You lit its fire once again,
Rather than soothe it, you stoked it with a knife,
What a wound, a deep bleeding wound.

> *My heart burns, my love,*
> *My harp and lyre have broken,*
> *You leapt beyond reach! Where did you go?*
> *Oh lord of my life, my master.*

As an orphan adrift without guidance,
I lived in the breeze of your shade,
Your love turned me into a nightingale
And I sang freely of love.

Are you so heartless to hate me?
How bad luck befell me already!
My love, you orphaned my heart,
And left me wandering aimless.

Սերից էրված

Սերից էրված պապակ սրտիս
Նորեն դուն էլ կրակ զարկիր,
Արնոտ վերքիս, խորունկ վերքիս,
Մահլամի տեղ դանակ զարկիր։

Վառավ, յա՛ր, սիրտս, ջիգյարս,
Կոտրվեց սազս, քնարս,
Չեռքես թռար, ու՞ր գնացիր,
Իմ կյանքիս տերը, սարդարըս։

Եթում էի հորից-մորից,
Շքիղ հովին էի ապրում,
Բլբուլ դառած, յա՛ր, քո էշխից,
Միշտ ազատ սեր էի երգում։

Ա՛խ, դու զալում, ինձ ատեցիր,
Ջաթի բախտից էի ատված,
Յա՛ր, քեզնից էլ որբ թողեցիր,
Ամեն ճամփես թողիր փակված։

We Are Not One

We are not one, do not open your breast,
Cease your torment, I will not endure,
Oh, so heartless and cruel, I am powerless and poor.

With your gorgeous body, your gleaming eyes,
Hearts melt under your gaze,
Under your eyebrow's arch, I burn for you,
Like a peacock draped in colours.

Anguishing with despair, please bring me some hope,
Approach me just once, so my sorrows can soothe,
Oh, so heartless and cruel, I am powerless and poor.

Քեզանից մաս չունիմ

Քեզանից մաս չունիմ, կուրծքդ մի՛ բանա,
Իզուր ինձ մի տանջիր, էլ չեմ դիմանա,
Անսիրտ, անշիգյար, խեղճ եմ, ապիկար։

Մարմինդ շբեղ, աչքերդ կանթեղ,
Սրտեր ես հալվում հայացքեդ ահեղ.
Ունքերդ կամար, էրվա քեզ համար.
Հազել ես նախշուն, դառել սիրամարգ։

Ջաթի ես հիվանդ եմ, քեզնեն ճար կուզեմ,
Մոտեցիր մեկ անգամ, դարդս քեզ ասեմ,
Անսիրտ, անշիգյար, խեղճ եմ, ապիկար։

Մարմինդ շբեղ, աչքերդ կանթեղ,
Սրտեր ես հալվում հայացքդ ահեղ.
Ունքերդ կամար, էրվա քեզ համար.
Հազել ես նախշուն, դառել սիրամարգ։

SHEET MUSIC

Դու իմ մուսան ես
You Are my Muse

Խոր մեծ ծովեր
Oh, Deep Vast Seas

Ջան, ջանիդ ղուրբան
Dear, Dear, My Dearest Love

Էսօր Արազն եւ գնացել
You Went To Araz Today

Սիրում եմ քեզ
I Love You

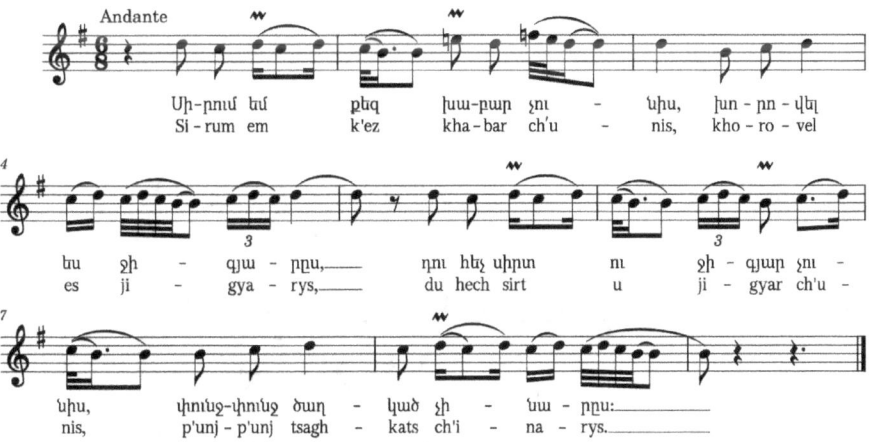

Մեկն էլ ես եմ շվարած
I Am The One, Stunned

Էս իմ սերն է
That's My Love

Մի բայա է
This Is My Sweetheart

Կոկոն վարդերի նման
Like Rose Buds

Սիրուն ես, հոգյակ
You Are Divine

Զով գիշեր է
It's A Cool Night

Մարալ ջան, հեզ արի
My Gazelle, Come Gently

Աղաւնաղ դուշ ես
You Are A Red Winged Dove

Սարեր կաղաչեմ
I Beg You Mountains

Ոլոր-մոլոր
I Became Lost

Էլի երկինքս ամպել է
My Sky Is Cloudy Again

Էլի էսօր սիրտս կուլա
My Heart Still Cries Today

Սիրունևեր
Beauties

Պարտիզում վարդեր բացված
In The Garden Roses Bloom

Աչրդ խումար
Your Beautiful Eyes

Նա մի նազ ունի
She Is In The Mood

Նա մի նազ ունի (շարուն.)
She Is In The Mood (contd.)

Թարլան, թարլան
Beautiful, Beautiful

Վարդ ցանեցի
I've Sowed A Rose

Անգութ դատաստան
Cruel Judgement

Թառը դոշիս
My Lute On My Chest

Հազար էրնեկ
I Wish It Was That Night

Սերից էրված
Burning From Love

Քեզանից մաաս չունիմ
We Are Not One

Քեզանից մաս չունիմ (շարուն.)
We Are Not One (contd.)

DICTIONARY OF GYUMRI DIALECT[7]

Ա

ԱՋԻԶ - Սիրելի, թանկագին: || Dear, sweetheart.
ԱԼԴԱՆԱԴ - Կարմիր թև ունեցող || Red winged.
ԱԼՎԱԼԱ - Կարմրավուն, գունագեղ: || Reddish, colorful.
ԱԼՎԱՆ - Երփներանգ, գույնզգույն, վառվռուն, հուրիրան: || Colorful, vibrant, fiery.
ԱԾԱԴ, ԱԶԱԲ - Արդյոք: || Whether.
ԱՆԳՅՈՒՄԱՆ - Անհույս, անհետ: || Hopeless, missing.
ԱՆԴԱԼԱԾ, ԱՆԴԱԼԱԹ - Անթերի, գեղեցիկ: || Perfect, beautiful.
ԱՆԴԱՆԱԴ - Անթև, թևեր չունեցող: Անդանադ դուշ՝ թևեր չունեցող աղավնի: || Wingless, who has no wings.
ԱՆԶԱԴ, ԱՆԶԱԽ - Հազիվ, հազիվհազ: Միայն թե: Սակայն, բայց: || Hardly, faintly.
ԱՆԶԻԳՅԱՐ - Անխիղճ, անսիրտ, անգութ: Սառը, անտարբեր: || Ruthless, heartless, cold, indifferent.
ԱՆՎԱԼԱԴ - Անփորձ, անհմուտ: || Inexperienced.
ԱՇԵԼ - Նայել, դիտել: || To look, to watch.
ԱՇՈՒԴ - Աշուղ են կոչվում ժողովրդական այն ստեղծագործողները, որոնք երգի խոսքն ու երաժշտությունը կատարում են որևէ երաժշտական գործիքի նվագակցությամբ (քամանչա, սազ, թառ և այլն): || Ashughs are the folk troubadours who performed the lyrics and music of a song with the accompaniment of a musical instrument (kamancha, saz, tar, etc.).
ԱՍԼԱՍ - Մետաքս, մետաքսե նուրբ գործվածք: || Silk, fine silk fabric.

---

[7] The following is a dictionary of words in Gyumri dialect (previously Alexandropol), which Sheram rely heavily on in his songs.

ԱՐՆԾՈՎ - Արյան ծով։ || Sea of blood.
ԱՐՈՒՍՅԱԿ - Արեգակի մոլորակներից մեկը (Վեներան), որ սովորաբար երևում է իբրև շատ պայծառ աստղ երեկոյան (Գիշերավար) կամ առավոտյան (Լուսաբեր, Լուսաստղ)։ || Venus.

Բ

ԲԱԶԱՐ - Շուկա։ || Market.
ԲԱԼԱՍԱՆ - Սպեղանի, դեղամիջոց, սփոփանք, մխիթարություն։ || Plaster, medicine, consolation, comfort.
ԲԱԼՔԻ - Գուցե, թերևս։ || Maybe.
ԲԱՂ - Այգի, բանջարանոց։ || Garden, vegetable garden.
ԲԱՂՉԱ, ԲԱԽՉԱ - Պարտեզ, այգի բանջարանոց։ || Garden, vegetable garden.
ԲԵԶԱՐԵԼ - Հոգնել, ձանձրանալ։ || To be tired or bored.
ԲԵԽԱԲԱՐ - Անտեղյակ, անիրազեկ։ || Unaware.
ԲԵՄՈՒՐԱԶ - Փափագը չկատարված, նպատակին չհասած, անմուրազ։ || The one who's desire has not been fulfilled.
ԲԵՉԱՐԱ - Անճարակ, խեղճ, թշվառ։ || Poor, miserable.
ԲԻՆԻՇ - Վերարկու, լայն ընդարձակ հագուստ-թիկնոց։ || Coat, wide loose clothing-cape.
ԲԼԲՈՒԼ - Սոխակ։ || Nightingale.
ԲԼԲՈՒԼ ԿՏՐԵԼ - Ոգևորված խոսել։ || To speak with excitement.
ԲԼԵԼ - Քանդվել, փուլ գալ։ || To crumble, to collapse.
ԲՈԲԼԻԿ - Ոտնաբոբիկ, ոտքերը մերկ։ || Barefoot.
ԲՈՒՍԱԽ - Ծնոտի տակի փափուկ միսը, ենթակզակ։ || The soft flesh under the chin.
ԲՈՒՉԱ - Շորերի կամ ուտելիքի կապոց։ || A bundle of clothes or food.
ԲՈՅ - Հասակի բարձրությունը, երկարություն։ || Height, stature.
ԲՈՅ ՈՒ ԲՈՒՍ(ԱԹ) - Լավ արտքին տեսք, բարձրահասակ ու գեղեցկատեմ։ || Someone with a good appearance, tall and handsome.
ԲՈՒԹԱ - Սիրելի, պաշտելի։ || Dear, adorable.

ԲՈՒԹԱ ՏԱԼ - Սիրելի էակի հետ համաձայնության գալ: || To come to an agreement with a loved one.
ԲՈՒՍՈՒՑԵԼ - Աճեցնել: || To grow.

Գ

ԳԵՂԱՆԱՁ - Գեղեցիկ նազանքով: || With beautiful tenderness.
ԳԵՂԳԵՂԵԼ - Դայլայլել, ձայնը խաղացնելով, կլկլացնելով երգել: || Singing with a quavering, warbling voice.
ԳՅՈՒՄԱՆ - Հույս: || Hope.
ԳՈՀԱՐ - Թանկագին, ազնիվ քար: Ազնվագույնը՝ լավագույնը իր տեսակի մեջ: || Precious, noble stone. The noblest, the best of its kind.

Դ

ԴԱԴԱՐԿՈՒՆ, ԴԱԴԱՐԳՅՈՒՆ - Ամեն ինչից զուրկ, տնից տեղից կտրված, թափառական դարձած: || Deprived of everything, cut off from home, wandered.
ԴԱՍՏԱ - Մի ձեռքում տեղավորվող քանակություն, փունջ, տրցակ, կապ: || Quantity to fit in one hand, bunch, bunch, tie.
ԴԱՐ - Բարձունք, լեռնալանջ, բլուր: Դարի դոշին՝ լեռան լանջին: || Hill, hillside, slope.
ԴԱՐԴ - Վիշտ, ցավ, հոգու մտահոգություն: || Sorrow, pain, worry.
ԴԱՐԴԱԺԱՐ - Հանգիստ՝ դադար չունեցող, անհանգիստ: || Restless.
ԴԱՐՄԱՆ - Դեղ, դեղամիջոց, սփոփանք, մխիթարություն: Դարդին դարման անել՝ հիվանդությունը՝ ցավը բուժելու համար միջոցներ գտնել: || Medicine, consolation. To cure the pain, to find the means to cure the disease, heartache.
ԴԻՎԱՆ - Դատ, դատաստան, դատարան: Դիվան անել՝ դատել, դատավճիռ կայացնել: || Trial, judgment, court.
ԴՈՇ - Կուրծք: Սարի՝ լեռան լանջ: || Breast. Slope.
ԴՈՇԱԿ - Ներքնակ, անկողին: || Mattress, bed.
ԴՈՒՄԱՆ - Մեգ, մշուշ, մառախուղ: Ծուխ, փոշի: || Fog, smoke, dust.

ԴՈՒՇՄԱՆ - Թշնամի։ || Enemy.

Ե

ԵԹՈՒՄ, ԵԹԻՄ - Որբ։ || Orphan.
ԵՇԻԼ - Նայել, տեսնել։ Սպասել։ || To look, to see.
ԵՐԴԻՔ, ԵՐԴԻԿ - Տանիք, հողե կտուր։ || Roof, earthen roof.

Զ

ԶԱԹԻ - Արդեն իսկ, հենց, ասենք։ || Just, already.
ԶԱԼՈՒՄ, ԶՈՒԼՈՒՄ - Աղետ, արհավիրք, պատուհաս, մեծ դժբախտություն։ || Disaster, catastrophe, plague, great misfortune.
ԶՄՐՈՒԽՏ - Վառ կանաչ գույնի թանկագին քար։ Կանաչ, կանաչ գույնի։ || Emerald. A bright green gemstone. Green, green color.

Է

ԷՆՉԱԽ - Այն ժամանակ։ || Then, at that time.
ԷՆՏԻ - Նորից, կրկին։ || Again.
ԷՇԽ - Սեր։ Եռանդ, ավյուն, ոգևորություն։ || Love. Energy, vigor, enthusiasm.
ԷՇԽԻ ԳԱԼ / ԸՆԿՆԵԼ - Ոգևորվել, խանդավառվել։ || Being excited, excited.
ԷՇԽ ՏԱԼ - Մեկի սիրտը սեր գցել։ || To fall in love.
ԷՐՎԵԼ - Վառվել, այրվել։ || To burn.

Ը

ԸՆՁԵՆ - Ինձանից։ || From me.
ԸՆՉԻ - Ինչու։ || Why?

Թ

ԹԱՌ - Աշուղների երաժշտական լարային գործիք: || Tar, a musical string instrument of ashughs.
ԹԱՌԼԱՆ - Շատ գեղեցիկ, չքնաղ: Բազե: || Very beautiful, wonderful. Falcon.
ԹԱՍ - Գավաթ, բաժակ, լայնաբերան ամա՞ն: || Cup, wide bowl.
ԹԱՔ - Մի հատիկ, միակ: || The only one, single.
ԹՎԱՆՔ - Հրացան: || A rifle.

Լ

ԼԱԶԱԹ - Հաճույք, բավականություն: || Pleasure, satisfaction.
ԼԱԼ - Շափյուղա: Թանկագին քար: || Sapphire.
ԼԱՆՋ - Կուրծք: Զառիվեր: || Breast. Slope.

Խ

ԽԱԲԱՐ - Լուր, տեղեկություն: || News, information.
ԽԱԹԱԲԱԼԱ - Գլխացավանք, հոգս: || Headache, concern.
ԽԱԺՈՒԺ - Կապտավուն կամ կանաչի տվող, խաժակն: Խաժ աչքերով: || A bluish or greenish hue (generally eyes). With squinting eyes.
ԽԱԼ - Բնածին մուգ գույնի նշան մարդու երեսի կամ մարմնի վրա: || A birthmark, nevus, mole.
ԽԱԼԻՍ - Մաքուր, զուտ, անխառն, իսկական: Խալիս ատլաս՝ իսկական մետաքս: || Clean, pure, unmixed, real.
ԽԱՆՉԱԼ - Դաշույն: || A dagger.
ԽԱՆԸՄ/ԽԱՆՈՒՄ - Տիկին: || Madam.
ԽԱՍ - Ընտիր, առաջնակարգ: Զուտ, անխառն, անարատ: Մետաքս, կերպաս: || Selected, first-class. Pure, unmixed, pure.
ԽԵՐ - Բարիք, բարերարություն: Բարի, լավ, հաջողակ, բարեզուշակ: Օգուտ, շահ: Փառք: || Good, charity. Kind, good, successful. Glory.

ԽՈՒՄԱՐ - Գեղեցկության հասնող, փոքր ինչ շիլ աչք ունեցող, անուշ հայացքով: Խումար աչք՝ Սիրունատես աչք, քիչ շիլ, գեղեցիկ աչքերով: || Beautiful, slightly flabby eyes, with a sweet look. A little shaggy, with beautiful eyes.

Ծ

ԾԱՎԻ - Բաց կապույտ, ծովագույն, երկնագույն: Կապուտացյա: || Light blue, navy blue.

Կ

ԿԱԼ - Հացահատիկի խուրձերը փռելու և կալսելու տեղ, կալատեղ: || A place to spread grains for threshing.
ԿԵՆԱԼ - Մնալ, լինել, գտնվել: || To stay, to be.
ԿԵՐՊԱՍ - Մետաքս, ատլաս: || Silk, satin.
ԿՈԼԽՈԶ - Կոլեկտիվ տնտեսություն: Գյուղատնտեսական ձևավորում Սովետական Միության ժամանակաշրջանում: || Collective farm. An agricultural farming unit during the Soviet era.
ԿՈՒԼԱՄ - Կլացեմ: || I will cry.

Հ

ՀԱԼԱԼ - Արդար, անխարդախ, ազնիվ: Հարազատ: Շիտտ, ուղիղ: || Fair, honest, straight.
ՀԱԼԱԼ-ՋՈՒԼԱԼ - Մաքուր, արդար: || Clean, pure, fair.
ՀԱԼԱՎ - Հագուստ, զգեստ, շոր: || Clothes, dress.
ՀԱԽԻՑ ԳԱԼ - Արժանի պատիժտ տալ, վրեժ լուծել: || To give a worthy punishment, to take revenge.
ՀԱՅԻԼ-ՄԱՅԻԼ ԿՏՐԵԼ - Զմայլվել, սքանչանալ: Խիստ զարմանալ, ապշել: || To admire, to marvel. To be very surprised.
ՀԱՆԴ - Դաշտ, արտ: || Field.

ՀԱՎԱՍ - Տրամադրություն, փափագ, իղձ: || Mood, desire, longing.
ՀԱՎՔ - Թռչուն: || A bird.
ՀԱՐԱՄ - Պիղծ, ապականված: Կեղտոտ, անմաքուր: Անարդար, անազնիվ: || Dirty, corrupt, unfair, dishonest.
ՀԵԳ - Խեղճ, թշվառ: || Miserable.
ՀԵԴ - Անգամ: Ինչ կայրե ամեն հեղի՝ ինչ կայրե ամեն անգամ: || Every time.
ՀԵՅՐԱՆ - Զմայլանք, հիացմունք: Հեյրան անել՝ խելքահան անել, խենթացնել: Հեյրան լինել՝ սքանչանալ, զմայլվել: || Admiration. To amaze, to drive crazy. To be admired.
ՀԵՔԻՄ - Տնական միջոցներով բուժող բժիշկ: || Homeopathic doctor.
ՀՆԱՐ - Հնարավորություն, ճար, կարելիություն: || Opportunity.

Ղ

ՂԱՆԱԴ - Թռչունի թև: Դռան պատուհանի փեղկ: || Bird's wing. Door or window sash.
ՂԱՆԱՎՈՒԶ - Մետաքսե ընտիր կտոր, կերպաս: || A fine piece of silk, satin.
ՂՈՒԼ - Ծառա: Ղուլ եղնիլ՝ ծառա դառնալ: || Servant. Slave.
ՂՈՒՇ - Աղավնի: Ընդհանրապես թռչուն: || A dove. Generally a bird.
ՂՈՒՐԲԱՆ ԵՂՆԻԼ - Մատաղ լինել, շատ սիրելուց պատրաստ լինել կյանքը զոհելու: || To be a sacrifice, to be willing to sacrifice life out of love.

Ճ

ՃԱՐ - Դեղ, դարման: Հնար: || Medicine.

Մ

ՄԱԼ ՈՒ ՄԱԼԱԼ - Իղձ, փափագ, եռանդ: || Desire, longing, energy.

ՄԱԼ ՈՒ ՄՈՒԼՔ - Մալ՝ խոշոր եղջերավոր անասուն, տավար: Մուլք՝ անշարժ գույք, կալվածք: Մալ ու մուլք՝ հարստություն, կարողություն: || Cattle, beef. Property, real estate, estate.

ՄԱԼՈՒԼ - Տխուր: || Sad.

ՄԱԼՈՒՄ - Հայտնի, նշմարելի, աչքի ընկնող: || Famous, noticeable, conspicuous.

ՄԱՀԼԱՄ - Սպեղանի, վիրակապ: || Bandage.

ՄԱՀՐՈՒՄ - Ձուրկ, զրկված: || benefit, interest.

ՄԱՅԱ - Օգուտ, շահ: || Benefit, interest, profit.

ՄԱՋՆՈՒՆ - Մերձավոր Արևելքում տարածված "Լեյլի և Մեջնուն" սիրավեպի հերոս: Համարժեք է "Ռոմեո և Ջուլիետ" սիրավեպի Ռոմեոյի կերպարին՝ սիրահար երիտասարդ: || The hero of the "Leyli and Mejnun" love epic popular in the Middle East. Equivalent to the image of Romeo in Shakespeare's "Romeo and Juliet", a young man in love.

ՄԱՐԱԼ - Եղնիկ, եղջերու: Շատ գեղեցիկ: || Deer. Very beautiful.

ՄԱՐՋԱՆ - Թանկագին քար, կորալ, բուստ: Ծովային պոլիպների մի տեսակ, որի կրացած մարմիններից գոյացած սպիտակ, կարմիր կամ սև գույնի քարերից հատուկ մշակմամբ զարդարանք են պատրաստում: || Precious stone, corall.

ՄԵՅԴԱՆ - Հրապարակ, ասպարեզ: || Square, arena.

ՄԸՇՀԱՆԱ, ՄԱՇԱՆԱ - Կեղծ պատճառ, չսչին պատճառաբանություն: Մահանա բռնել՝ պատճառ, առիթ որոնել: || False reason. To look for a reason, an occasion.

ՄՇԱԿ - Աշխատավոր, վարձու բանվոր, հողագործ, բեռնակիր: || Workman, farmer, porter.

ՄՈՅԻՔՈՒԼ - Ամուսնության գործերում միջնորդ կին: || A marriage mediator.

ՄՈՒՐԱԶ - Նվիրական ցանկություն, իղձ, փափագ: Մուրազին հասնել՝ նպատակին հասնել: Մուրազը փորը մնալ՝ նվիրական, տենչած ցանկությունը չհասած: || Sacred desire, longing.

Յ

ՅԱՂՈՒԹ - Սուտակ, հակինթ: Երկնագույն կամ դեղնակարմիր թանկագին քար, որ գործածում են որպես ակնեղեն: || Hyacinth. Blue or yellow-red precious stones used as gems.

ՅԱՄԱՆ -Խնդրանքի՝ աղաչանքի բացականչություն, oh, աղաչում եմ: Սոսկալի, սարսափելի: Դժվար, ծանր: Մեծ, հսկայական: Վշտի՝ ցավի բացականչություն: Յաման յարա՝ անբուժելի վերք: || The cry of supplication. An outcry of sorrow.

ՅԱՆԴՈՒՆ - Հրդեհ: Կրակոտ, վառվռուն: || Fire. Fiery.

ՅԱՐ - Սիրած աղջիկ կամ տղա, սիրուհի, սիրեկան: || Mistress, lover.

ՅԱՐԱ - Վերք, հոգեկան տառապանք, վիշտ, ցավ: Յարա շինել՝ վերք դարձնել: || Wound, mental suffering, sorrow, pain.

ՅԱՐԱԼՈՒ - Վիրավոր, վերք ունեցող: Վշտահար, վիշտ՝ ցավ ունեցող: || Wounded.

ՅԱՐԱՆ - Բարեկամ, ընկեր: Օգնող, աջակից: Յարանը յարա կը բանա՝ մարդուն ցավ պատճառողը ընկերը՝ բարեկամն է լինում: || Friend. Supporter.

ՅՈՐԴԱՆ - Վերմակ: || Blanket.

Ն

ՆԱԶ - Կոտրատվելը, չեմուչում: Նազանք, պչրանք, կոկետություն, քնքշանք: Նազ անել՝ չեմուչում անել, ձևացնել թե չի ուզում: || Coquetry.

ՆԱԶԱՏԱՐ - Նազերը տանող: Չեմուչում անելուն, կոտրատվելուն դիմացող մարդ: || A person who resists to someone's coquetry.

ՆԱԶԱՐ - Չար աչք: Չտան նազար՝ աչքով չտան: || Evil eye.

ՆԱԶԼՈՒ - Գեղեցիկ, վայելչագեղ, նազելի: || Beautiful, elegant, graceful.

ՆԱՄԱՐԴ - Տմարդի, անազնիվ, ստոր մարդ: || A dishonest, insidious man.

ՆՈՃԻ - Բարձր՝ սլացիկ ու նրբագեղ հասակ։ Նոճազգիների ընտանիքին պատկանող մշտադալար ծառ։ || Tall, slender and elegant. Evergreen tree.

Շ

ՇԱՀԱՆ - Բազե։ Շահանի աչքեր՝ մեծ աչքեր։ || Falcon. Falcon eyes, big eyes.

ՇԱՀՄԱՐ - Սև ու ողորուն, օձանման։ Օձի առանձին տեսակ, որ ավելի մեծ է և կարմիր գույն ունի։ || Winding, like a snake.

ՇԱՂ - Բարակ անձրև, ցող կաթիլ։ || Thin rain, dew drop.

ՇԱՄԱՄ - Ոչ շատ մեծ, գնաղածն անուշահոտ սեխ։ Նմանությամբ ասվում է մատաղատի աղջիկների համար։ Շամամի նման կլոր՝ գեղեցիկ ու հոտավետ։ || Not too big, round and fragrant melon. Round like shamam, beautiful and fragrant.

ՇԱՎԱՂ/ՇԱՓԱՂ - Փայլ, շող, ցոլք, լույս։ || Shine, shine, glare, light.

ՇԱՐՄԱՂ - Գեղեցիկ, սիրուն։ Բարակ, նազով, նուրբ։ || Beautiful, lovely. Thin, delicate.

ՇԻՏԿԵԼ - Ուղղել, դարձնել։ || To correct.

ՇԼՎԱ - Մատաղաշ տունկի, շիվ։ Բարձր ու բարակ, բարնձն, ճկուն։ || Sampling. Tall and thin,, flexible.

ՇՈՐՈՐԱԼ - Նազանքով շարժվել, սիգաճեմ քայլել։ || To move gracefully, to walk slowly.

ՇՈՒԽ - Աշխույժ, զվարթ, կենսուրախ։ || Lively, cheerful.

ՇՎԱՐ - Շվարած, շփոթված. մոլորված։ || Stunned, confused, lost.

Զ

ԶԱԹԻՆ - Դժվար։ || Difficult.

ԶԱՅ - Գետ։ Զայի ափի՝ գետի ափի։ || River.

ԶԱՐԱ - Հույս, ապավեն։ Ճար, հնար։ *Զարա բեշարա՝ ճարահատյալ, ճարը կտրած։* || Hope, reliance.

ԶԻՐՔԻՆ - Sգեղ։ || Ugly.

ՉՈԼ - Անապատ, անշրդի, անմշակ տարածություն: Վայրի՝ անբնակ տեղ: || Desert, arid, uncultivated space. Wild, uninhabited place.
ՉՈԼԻ ՋԵՅՐԱՆ - Վայրի եղնիկ: || Wild deer.
ՉՈՒԼ ՈՒ ՓԱԼԱՍ - Հին ու մին, հնացած, մաշված, անպետքացած զգեստ: || Old, worn, or useless dress.
ՉՓԼԱԴ - Մերկ, տկլոր, աղքատ: || Naked, poor.

Պ

ՊԱԼԱ - Բալա, որդի, որդյակ: || Dear.
ՊԵԽ - Բեղ: || Moustache.

Ջ

ՋԱՆ - Մարմին, կյանք: Գործածվում է գոյականների հետ իբրև փաղաքշական բառ՝ սիրելիս, հոգիս իմաստով: || Body, life. Usually, added to names or nouns to express affection, for example: Emushok jan, Arusik jan, David jan.
ՋԵԲ - Գրպան: || Pocket.
ՋԵՅՐԱՆ - Այծյամի կամ կխտարի մի տեսակ, գեղեցիկ կազմվածքով, եղջերու, վիթ: Բարեկազմ, բարեձև՝ ճկուն մարմին ունեցող, վայելչակազմ, ջեյրանի նման (աղջիկ, պատանի): || A kind of deer, gazelle. Slim, slender, with a flexible body, elegant.
ՋԻԳՅԱՐ - Սիրելի, մտերիմ, սրտակից: Գութ, խիղճ, հարազատի նկատմամբ սրտակցություն: || Dear, close, cordial.
ՋԻՎԱՆ - Երիտասարդ, ջահել: || Young.
ՋՈԿ ՄՆԱԼ - Առանձին մնալ, առանձնացած լինել: || Stay separate, be separate.
ՋՈՐԵԼ - Խռովել, նեղանալ: || To be upset, to be offended.
ՋՈՒԽՏԱԿ - Զույգ, երկվորյակ: || Couple, twins.
ՋՈՒԴԱԲ - Լուր, տեղեկություն: Պատասխան: || News, information.

U

ՍԱԶ - Արևելյան լարային նվագարան։ || String instrument of ashughs.

ՍԱԼԹ - Հենց, միմիայն, միայն։ || Exactly, only.

ՍԱՂ - Ամբողջ, ողջ։ || Alive, all.

ՍԱՉԵՐ - Երկար հյուսավոր մազեր։ || Long braided hair.

ՍԱՎԴԱ - Սեր։ || Love.

ՍԱՎԴԱԼՈՒ - Սիրահար, սիրուց տարված։ || Lover, obsessed with love.

ՍԱՐԴԱՐ - Գլխավոր, մեծ։ || Chief, big.

ՍԵԳ - Դար, բլրոտ, սեղ տեղ։ || A hill.

ՍԵՅՐ ԱՆԵԼ - Նայել, դիտել։ || To watch.

ՍԵՅՐԱՆ - Ման գալը, զբոսնելը, զբոսանք։ Զբոսնելու հաճելի, գեղեցիկ ու հովասուն տեղ։ || A pleasant, beautiful and airy place to walk.

ՍԵՖԻԼ, ՍԵՓԻԼ - Թռչունների ձայն՝ աղմուկ։ Սեֆիլ բայաթի՝ արևելյան մի եղանակ։ || The sound of birds - noise. Sefil bayati, a type of eastern melody.

ՍԻՊԵՂ/ՍԻԲԵԽ - Հովանոցավորների ընտանիքին պատկանող բանջարաբույս։ || A type of edible wild plant.

ՍՄԲՈՒԼ - Կապույտ թերթիկներով սարի հոտավետ ծաղիկ։ Ընդհանուր անուն տարբեր անուշահոտ ու գույնզգույն ծաղիկների։ || A fragrant mountain flower with blue leaves. Common name for various fragrant and colorful flowers.

ՍՅՈՒՐԵ, ՍՈՒՐԱՀԻ - Երկար վզով կավե ամաև՝ գինու, օղու, ջրի և այլ հեղուկների համար։ Բարակ՝ նուրբ ու երկար, բարձրուղեշ։ *Սյուրեի կլոր մեջքդ՝ նուրբ ու երկար մեջքդ։* || A long-necked clay vessel for wine, vodka, water and other liquids. Thin, delicate and long, high-pitched.

ՍՈՅ - Տեսակ։ Տոհմ, ցեղ։ || Type. Dynasty, tribe.

ՍՈՎԴԱՔՅԱՐ - Սիրահար։ || Lover.

ՍՈՒՐՄԱ - Կապույտ դեղ, որը կանայք քսում են աչքերին, ծարիր։ || Antimony, a blue colored cosmetic that women apply to their eyes, try it.

Վ

ՎԱԹԱՆ - Հայրենիք, հայրենի երկիր: || Homeland, native country.
ՎԱԽԹ - Ժամանակ: || Time.
ՎԵՐԱՆԱ - Ամայի, անմարդաբնակ, ավերակ:
ՎՌՇՆԵԼ - Պտտվել, ման գալ: || To ramble, stroll.

S

ՏԵՅՄՈՐ(Ի) - Մինչև որ: || Until.
ՏՆԿՈՁԱՆԱԼ - Տարամադրությունը բարձրանալ (խմիչքից): Զուգվել - զարդարվել: || Slightly intoxicated, tipsy, tiddly (mostly from alcohol).

ՈՒ

ՈՒՄՈՒՏ, ՈՒՄՈՒԴ - Հույս: || Hope.

Փ

ՓԱԼԱՍ - Հատակին փռելու հասարակ կարպետ: || A simple floor carpet.
ՓԱՐԱ - Փող, դրամ: || Money.
ՓԵՇ - Զգեստի քղանցք: Լեռան ստորոտ: || The hem of the dress. At the foot of the mountain.
ՓԵՐԻ - Իգական սեռի առասպելական բարի ոգի: Զբնադագեղ՝ չնաշխարհիկ կին՝ աղջիկ: || A mythical kind spirit of a female. Wonderful, unworldly woman, girl.
ՓՆՋԻԿ - Փունջ: || Bunch.

Ք

ՔԹՈՑ - Ոստերից հյուսած խոր ու մեծ զամբյուղ: || A deep and large basket made of vines.

ՔՅԱՐԱՄ - "Ասլի և Քյարամ" արևելյան ժողովրդական երգախառն սիրավեպի հերոս: || The hero of the "Asli and Kyaram" folk love epic.

ՔՅԱՐԳԱՀ/ՔԱՐԳԱՀ - Փայտե շրջանակ, որի մեջ ձգված ամրացնում են կտորը՝ վրան ասեղնագործելու համար: || A wooden frame with a piece of stretched cloth for embroidery.

ՔՅԱՐՎԱՆ - Քարավան: || Caravan.

ՔՆԱՐ - Հին լարավոր երաժշտական գործիք, որ նվագում էին մատներով կամ փոքրիկ փղոսկրյա փայտիկով: || An old stringed musical instrument played with the fingers or a small ivory stick.

Ֆ

ՖԻՏԱՆ/ՖԻԴԱՆ - Երիտասարդ, գեղահասակ: || Young, handsome.

ALSO AVAILABLE

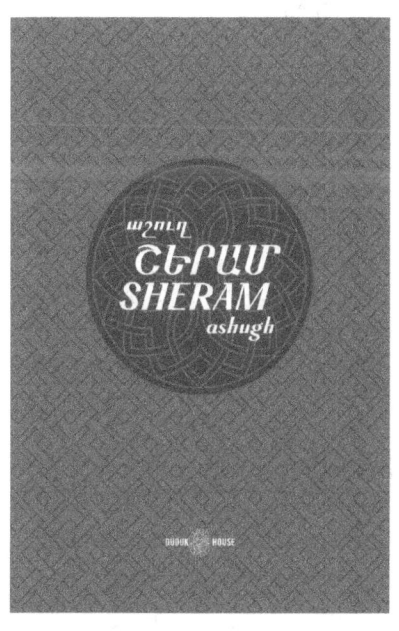

Sheram: Songs with music notation in Armenian and transliterated English lyrics (Armenian Ashoughs)

It is with great pleasure that we announce the publication of complete collection of Armenia's most important ashoughs' works in transliterated English for the first time in history. More than 100 songs of Sheram are included in this book, each with a music notation and Armenian lyrics transliterated into English. There are five chapters in the book: Love Songs, From the Sad Past, Satirical, Dances, and Appendix. The first four chapters of this book contain transcriptions of songs written by Sheram's son, composer Vardges Talyan circa 1948. There are also transcriptions of several songs by another scholar, musicologist Aram Kocharyan.

This book ends with transcriptions of the most popular songs of Sheram, as performed by two of his greatest interpreters, Araksya Gyulzadyan and Ofelia Hambardzumyan.

- **Publisher:** Dudukhouse (August 27, 2022)
- **Language:** English
- **Paperback:** 300 pages
- **ISBN-13:** 978-1777999032

Buy it on Amazon: https://www.amazon.com/Sheram-notation-Armenian-transliterated-Ashoughs/dp/1777999030

TABLE OF CONTENTS

FROM THE PUBLISHER	1
TO THE UNFORGETTABLE MEMORY OF THE POET-SINGER SHERAM	4
A COUPLE OF WORDS	6
SONG LYRICS	15
SHEET MUSIC	77
DICTIONARY OF GYUMRI DIALECT	111
TABLE OF CONTENTS	128

Sheram In Love

*A colorful collection of love songs
from one of Armenia's most notable ashoughs*

Editor in Chief	Armen Matosyan
Poetry Editor	Daniel Roca
Calligraphy	Ruben Malayan
Cover Design	Armen Matosyan

© Dudukhouse, 2022
www.dudukhousemusic.com

www.ingramcontent.com/pod-product-compliance
Lightning Source LLC
Chambersburg PA
CBHW050252120526
44590CB00016B/2313